SENSITIVE WARRIOR

10 Ways to Respond When You're Called "Overly Sensitive"

Unblock Your Voice

WRITTEN & EDITED BY

JULIA ROSE WILD, M.S.

Copyright

you in life. However, we do not purport this as a "quick fix methodology" and there is no guarantee that you will experience life changes or results by using the techniques discussed in this book. The intent of the author is only to offer information of a general nature to help you in your quest for emotional and spiritual well-being. No guarantees, promises, representations, or warranties of any kind regarding specific or general benefits, personal development, or otherwise, have been or will be made by the author. The author cannot guarantee your success, ability to change your life, and specifically do not make any such representations. Any personal growth changes outlined in this book, or any material or statements disseminated by the author in any way, is simply their experience-based expectations for future potential and thus not promises for actual performance. These statements are simply derived from the author's opinions, observations, and/or experience. In the event you use any of the information in this book for yourself, which is your constitutional right, the author makes no guarantees that you will achieve any particular results from the book's information, and is not responsible for your actions and results in business or in life.

Cover designed by the author via Canva.com

ISBN: 978-1-7345299-2-0 (Print)
ISBN: 978-1-7038-0213-9 (Kindle)
ASIN: B07ZR5LBWZ

Library of Congress Control Number: 2020901111

For the autistic children.

TABLE OF CONTENTS

Acknowledgments

I thank my cat Seraphina, who is named after 6-winged angels (I thank them too). She has taught me so much about self-possession and unconditional love. I thank every friend, mentor and connection who has supported and inspired me. Your kindness, funnies and encouragement have meant the world to me. Same to the divine multiverse and all who look out for me.

I thank every brave, sensitive soul who is committed to staying that way in a harsh world and not giving up. And, I thank whoever invented cauliflower pizza crust.

Writing this book is a dream come true! It's been a challenging run for me. The fact that I'm here to write this is miraculous. I can't help but feel thankful for that, and you reading it. May the words in this book provide upliftment and empowerment to those who read it, as many have done for me. And make you laugh here and there. Love and light.

Author's Note

My upbringing was not the kind that encouraged having a healthy sense of self and asserting it. Especially if you were female. I even remember once having a nightmare in which one of my parents shot me in the throat with a gun.

This book reflects a piece of my path back from that. Back to myself. Like all individuals who are oppressed in one way or another, the spark of your soul continues to feel that discomfort, and seeks to be known. To be expressed. We all want to be understood.

There's nothing wrong with wanting to stop sensitivity shaming. People who are highly sensitive and/or empathic can have a particularly tough time when it comes to speaking up about it. This book is for you.

The kind of consciousness we bring hasn't always been embraced, but I do believe that's shifting.

Sensitivity is needed and valuable. I'm not saying it's superior. I'm saying it's equal and important. You will hear me repeat affirmative statements about it throughout the book, because I aim to saturate you in delicious self-confidence.

I decided to write about 10 ways to respond to being called "overly sensitive" because this question came up over and over again from highly sensitive people: "What do I say when people call me overly sensitive, or tell me to stop being so sensitive?"

I've experienced sensitivity shaming, and crafted effective replies to set boundaries in my life. Note: This isn't intended as a book on resolving conflict. It's to help with confidence and having words to address sensitivity shaming (though you'd hope one would lead to the other). Of course, no one can guarantee results. I can say that most of the 10 responses provided have been real-life tested by yours truly, with positive effect. The rest have come to me through others. Sometimes simply having the words to say can be hugely helpful. The stories I share are to illustrate concepts and convey that you're not alone.

The single greatest factor to fire-up your voice is your unshakable confidence in who you are and what you bring. Some of what I write is to help support you in working through personal material that might be in the way of that.

Confidence comes from two latin words: "Con" (meaning *with*) and "fidere" (meaning *faith* or *trust)*. In essence, it means to trust yourself. I would love for readers to complete this book feeling happy and secure in being sensitive. With more faith and trust in who you are. I hope you end this book feeling empowered with specific words, and confident that sensitivity, and the awareness it brings, are needed and valuable gifts. Because they truly are.

You are a cosmically orchestrated miracle. The odds of you being here, as the unique person you are, are about 1 in 400 billion. So don't tell me you shouldn't be sensitive, or any other way you came in. Don't let anyone else tell you either.

You are wonderful, powerful and beautiful.

PART 1

GOOD BYE KITTY

I don't like Hello Kitty®. I know that probably sounds like a demented way for a sensitive cat-lover to start a book on unblocking your voice, but hear me out. No shade intended towards this internationally beloved icon. I simply don't like when a veritable emblem of girlish cuteness is portrayed without a mouth. Have you ever noticed that? She's accompanied an untold number of children into adulthood, and is adorable. Yet often in still frame caricatures and dolls, does not have a mouth. If you don't have a mouth, how can you have a voice? I do not approve of this message. I encourage you to have a voice.

It is an intense and special time for human consciousness on earth. I believe what sensitives bring is crucial to the time at hand - Equally as much as the valuable contributions anyone is making, as we clear out the old and bring in the new.

Sensitives observe and register a great many things. You and your voice are needed and important. Sometimes honoring this means setting clear, appropriate boundaries with those who attempt to shame you for this beautiful quality.

To reiterate, I will be belaboring this point throughout the book. I aim to offset some of the negativity and disenfranchisement around the quality of being sensitive. Because often times, it's the sense that one is "less than" or not worthy that can stop you from setting appropriate boundaries.

Putting a stop to sensitivity shaming by asserting boundaries is healthy. Whether you're funny or fierce when you set them, it's important to set them. I invite you to get comfortable with the idea of using your voice to assert your right to be sensitive. To get comfortable with owning your empowered voice. It's time to say "Good bye kitty. Hello voice". Me-ow.

YOUR VOICE MAKES BABIES

Your voice is a powerful force of creation. You are emitting vibration, combined with will and intent, out into the world which, in turn, can influence the creation of realities in that world. You can use it for good or evil, relation or disconnection, singing or burping, ordering fries with or without cheese. The creative potential is enormous. It's important to use it responsibly.

I'll put it another way. For a period of time in my early 20s, I was fixated on studying Western astrology. I learned that each sign has a polarity (an opposite sign) on the wheel of astrological signs. Each sign also has an associated body part and physical function. Opposing signs can be understood as having a complimentary relationship and energies. Similar in degree but different in expression (think "opposites attract").

In astrology, the throat and voice are associated with the sign of Taurus (the bull). The opposite sign of Taurus is Scorpio (the scorpion). Scorpio rules the reproductive organs. It rules physical and metaphysical regeneration including sexual reproduction - One of the most powerful and primal creative urges. Without it, we'd have no life.

One way of understanding the connection between Taurus (and the throat), and Scorpio (and the reproductive organs) is to see the power of one's voice as having equal creative power to the act of reproduction.

This places the creative power of using one's voice on par the most essential procreative act, which results in making life. Your voice can seed realities and new life into existence. In other words, your voice makes babies. Existential babies. So grab a stroller and rainbow plushy because we be changing diapers.

WHY IT'S IMPORTANT FOR SENSITIVES TO SPEAK UP

I've come to appreciate my voice because I was someone who used to have the hardest time saying "no" to anything. In fact, I wasn't much aware "no" was an option. I practically felt my lot in life was to over-give and tolerate unkind, crappy behavior, because that's essentially what had been familiar.

As time passed and adulting happened, life became more complex. I learned in a visceral way that there was a real cost to not speaking up, in every area of my life. It caused me upset and distraction. For example, sometimes it led me to either stay in unhealthy dynamics longer than was good for me or I'd withdraw from some people entirely. Or I would think about a situation repeatedly, without seeing a way through it using words. This led to resentment, and a feeling of helplessness. All because I did not know how to speak into healthy confrontation or self-assertion.

Some may associate "confrontation" with aggression, but to me it doesn't have that overtone. It simply means to face someone or something, rather than pretend a problem doesn't feel like a pebble in your shoe. If that word doesn't work for you, feel free to insert whatever term puts speaking up in an empowering light.

As a highly sensitive person (HSP), the "pebble in shoe" feeling can be heightened and prolonged, which is why using your voice matters. It's also important to use your voice because we can get an inordinate amount of shaming for this wonderful quality that is an essential part of who we are. It's challenging to notice more and simultaneously be given the message that we shouldn't. It can shut you down.

When you start to treat yourself better than the people who shut you down by doing the opposite and encouraging yourself, healing happens. You stop seeking or needing approval and permission from others to be who you are, and who you want to be.

Things like conflict, difficult emotions and discordant energies can impact us more deeply. There are many studies now that speak to the negative impact of emotional repression on health, and that showcase how expression positively impacts wellness. By lovingly providing ourselves opportunities to assert ourselves in the world, we also speak our value and equality into it. And you never know how your words may positively impact another person.

Sometimes you want to correct the prejudice of those who errantly presume sensitivity is caused by trauma or poor parenting. No one likes being told who they are is a symptom.

There is nothing wrong with you. You are who you are, as you are, for perfect reasons. It is your birthright to be sensitive, feel what you feel, and to protect yourself with appropriate words when that birthright is shamed.
No one else will do it for you.

I'll also share that as I spoke up more, and learned other techniques to clear and ground myself, I felt less codependent and more at ease with myself and others.

PART 2

YOU'RE ALREADY A WARRIOR

I was in my 20s when I learned the term "highly sensitive person". As I read Dr. Elaine Aron's book on the subject, a part of me felt like I had finally arrived and been seen. Her book "normalized" qualities about me that had previously left me wondering if I was a hawk that had accidentally been put in a human body - Owing to keen sensory awareness, not flight ability. I wish.

According to Dr. Aron, HSPs have more sensitive nervous systems and deeper processing compared to non-HSPs. They are often more sensitive to scents, noises, violence and other environmental stimuli. If you're not sure you're an HSP, you can go to her site and take a brief quiz. In her book, Dr. Aron states that up to 20% of the population is wired up this way. However, these days, I think the number is higher.

This world can be quick to dismiss sensitivity. It's either "Well, everyone is sensitive" or "Stop being so sensitive". But those who think everyone is sensitive aren't giving high sensitivity proper discernment. They may not understand the nervous system research, deeper processing and other unique qualities that accompany high sensitivity. Besides, do they really know "everyone"? How do you have time to meet 7 billion people?

Again, I'm not saying high sensitivity is superior or inferior. I'm affirming that it IS. If you're HSP, chances are you were born that way. If it were any other inherent human quality, from sexual orientation to hair color to skin color to physical ability, shaming you about those things would be unacceptable. I don't see sensitivity shaming as any different.

I don't consider high sensitivity to be pathology, or a symptom of pathology, as some do. Sometimes society has a funny way of marginalizing differences. To me, that would be like saying blond hair is pathological because I'm a brunette. It's just different. And within that, each HSP is unique.

I'll add that, in my opinion, based on my research and experience, people who mistake high sensitivity as a symptom of trauma are misinformed. There is a difference between qualities of deep processing, versus symptoms of nervous system dysregulation.

While it's not without its challenges, sensitivity is a wonderful trait that can come with remarkable intuitive gifts. It often means you are highly perceptive and detect subtle, important things others miss.

Plug-in air fresheners are a good example. I tried them when they first came out. I couldn't put my finger on it, but there was something about them that registered as irritating and made me feel uneasy. Eventually research came out about phthalates in them, which is a substance that has potentially been linked to asthma, birth defects, organ damage and other issues.

There are many examples of this kind of early awareness in my life. I share this to highlight one of the valuable aspects of high sensitivity, in a world that can undervalue this trait. Also because

I'm guessing people can relate, and I want you to know you're not alone.

Later, I also learned what an "empath" was, and other experiences in my life that hadn't made much sense finally started making sense. This book is focused on high sensitivity, so I'm not going to go into being an empath. Not all HSPs are empaths (and vice versa). However, both sensitivity and empathic ability are highly sensate gifts, and I mention this because high sensitivity can come with energetic awareness. Another valuable gift.

I'm sure you got the memo that everything is essentially made of energy. Being able to deeply sense and tune into it can give a person valuable insight. It can provide a kind of literacy into people and events that many often secretly wonder about. One HSP I met said she could feel other peoples' intentions. And when it comes to creativity, the ability to play with translating the energy of words into images or sound is pure joy.

So why do I say you're already a warrior? Sometimes sensitivity is mistaken as a kind of weakness, but I believe very much to the contrary.

For a time, I was hesitant to fully own this beautiful quality. When I thought about why, it came down to conditioning.

There are stereotypes associated with sensitivity. That it not only suggests you're weak, but also potentially over-reactive, constantly crying into a blanket, or in need of reassurance. Maybe you think I need a binky.

There's an aspect of our society that seems to like people to be "tough". We mistake it for strength. This concept of "tough" can include near callous levels of self-interest, and seeking happiness through externals, sometimes at other peoples' expense. However, I've found that sometimes "tough" can be a mask that covers-up what's really going on, or a way to hide from genuine emotions. In my book (which you're literally reading right now), tough and strong are different. Tough can be a form of avoidance. The choice to be vulnerable and real takes strength.

When I sat quietly with it, I realized that conditioned beliefs about sensitivity weren't my beliefs about sensitivity. They were other people's. People I don't even know. Maybe even dead people. And I didn't agree with them. I don't think tough is better. And gentleness can be powerful.

Sensitivity and strength are often polarized or perceived as mutually exclusive, but they're not. For the record, I've known plenty of non-HSP people who've been big criers, and needed a lot of reassurance (I lent them my binky). I've also met HSPs who are very sensitive in terms of sense perception, but not so interpersonally sensitive. Unsurprisingly, stereotypes don't make much sense. Categorizing people is for convenience, not accuracy.

When I cut through the conditioning, I realized sensitivity is beautiful and valuable to me. That I enjoy being sensitive. If anything, I feel most of the world isn't sensitive enough. If I were the betting kind, I'd be willing to bet that more problems have been caused by lack of sensitivity, than the presence of it.

I saw that to be sensitive in this world is to already be a warrior, and to already be fierce. It often comes with intensity, which isn't for those lacking strength. You also need to be very strong and patient to come with these gifts, in a world that's been rather insensitive. That can fight you simply for noticing things you can't help but notice. Or for feeling things you can't help but feel. I do believe this is changing. Part of creating that change is challenging the conditioning, and demanding the right to be the wonderful sensitives we are.

Along those lines, here are some exploratory questions for you to play with:

*What messages/conditioning did you receive about sensitivity?
*If you hadn't received them, what beliefs would you have about it based on your actual experience of sensitivity?
*Do you believe it's possible to be sensitive and strong at the same time?
*What does strong look like to you?
*Where are you at with embracing your sensitive warrior?

I invite you to get curious. To relish exploring your inner world, like you're an adventurer of your own soul and it's most beautiful place you could ever be. It is.

LORD OF THE VOICE

As I became armed with knowledge of terms such as HSP, empath and more, though it wasn't intentional, part of my path became reclaiming and cultivating my voice. The journey was neither immediate nor easy. It involved a harrowing trek with my bff, through snowy mountain passes into fiery pits of lava. Somewhere along the way we lost a wizard, there were black dragons flown by dead kings who tried to eat me alive, and a stalker in a thong who bit off my finger.

Actually, assertiveness can be challenging for anyone. We're kind of brainwashed not to be individuals.

One of the first times I decided to confront a supervisor was at a restaurant job many years ago. He'd had an angry outburst that crossed the line for me.

I remember my voice shaking as I started talking to him, nervous I'd get fired for bringing it to his attention and letting him know how I felt. But we got through it and the particular behavior I brought to his attention stopped. There were certainly peaks and valleys along my journey, but speaking up became easier.

Here's another thing to keep in mind. Of course your experience may be different, but I once heard that starting to be assertive is like turning on a water hose after a long period of non-use. What happens when you do that? Usually there's brown, stagnant water that purges first and you end up spraying it all over, as you unkink the neglected hose.

When you start to vocalize years of repressed feelings and words, you may find that you're more aggressive than assertive. Or you might be so used to tip-toeing around other people's feelings that your words are so vague, the other party needs a decryption team to understand you.

My point is that it's likely you'll make mistakes, and to give yourself compassion and grace when you do. We can all relate to the ups and downs of learning curves. Sometimes they turn into learning loops or learning connect-the-dots.

If there is a particularly strong emotional charge present or you're nervous before having a conversation, a few ways that can help get you clear and grounded are to imagine how you want to feel when the conversation is over (as well as how you'd like the other person to feel, if you'd like), and reverse engineer what you say from there. Other possibilities are to write out any strong charges first, and/or practice with a supportive person. Hey, there are a lot worse things you could be doing on a Wednesday night.

SELF-DISCOVERY & RECAP

Ready to roll up your sleeves and do some self-discovery? Too bad, we're doing it anyway. Why am I so adamant about this? Mindset around being sensitive, and boundary-setting are crucial. Especially around shaming, which David Hawkins, MD, PhD, describes as the lowest vibrating emotion. Someone can always find a decentl way to bring something up to you, but starting off with shame is lame.

The more confident you are, and the more you appreciate who you truly are and what you bring, the less shame can take. The more empathy you have for yourself, the less shame can take. Also, the more you see boundary-setting as healthy, the more you will appreciate setting them.

Not feeling you can be assertive can be tied to matters of self-worth or self-esteem. If you feel you don't deserve the right to be who you are, or assert boundaries, you're less likely to (another reason for my affirmations throughout the book). It can also be related to conditioning - Especially for women - about people-pleasing and not rocking the boat.

Here are a few questions to get some awareness flowing about your current relationship to assertiveness. I invite you to set aside at least a good 30 minutes with your favorite pen and notebook, or computer screen. Maybe light some incense or get some tea, as you prepare internal and external space to receive your truth.

My recommendation is to go with your first answer and not edit yourself in any way. Forget about grammar, punctuation, that 8th grade English teacher who took red pen to your essays like Jackson Pollock took paint to canvas. There's no right or wrong, we're looking for your truth. Let your stream of consciousness babble and flow:

*What stops you from speaking up when you've experienced sensitivity shaming? Dig deep.

*Can you think of 3 times in your life where you've set a boundary and it's gone well, or seen someone else do it and it's gone well?

*What are your beliefs about speaking up and setting boundaries? Saying "no"?

*Do you honor your sensitivity, and believe it's your birthright and a valuable gift? If not, how come?

*Why do you think people resort to sensitivity shaming? What is the emotional toll it takes on you when you don't speak up about it?

*Is the way you're currently asserting yourself in the world congruent with who you want to be?

*If there was something you were getting out of not owning your power, and not speaking your truth now, what would that be?

*Have you ever seen a boat NOT rock? A boat that doesn't rock would be a pretty lousy boat.

The penultimate question on the list is there because sometimes we don't realize there's a conditioned or unconscious pattern or payoff to limiting behaviors.

For example, avoiding speaking up may perpetuate a belief that you don't deserve more or better. It can keep you in a familiar zone, instead of poking your head above the pit and exploring what you really want, and who you truly are (i.e. beyond identities assigned to you, or projected upon you by people in your past).

Sometimes we sacrifice parts of ourselves to fit-in or just survive, but we keep making those decisions past the point where it served us. As a result, we can lose our sense of who we truly are. I'm not saying these examples necessarily apply to you, but I've found it's interesting to consider.

You're doing great. You're wonderful and your gifts are needed.

In summary, we've established 3 essential principles of speaking up, and can start to get to the 10 ways to respond when you're called "overly sensitive".

To recap, the 3 essential principles of speaking up are: 1) You have a powerful voice. Your voice makes babies. It's a power to be used responsibly. 2) Sensitivity is a wonderful, valuable gift. You are just as you should be. Being you is your birthright.

3) If/when your sensitivity is shamed, respecting yourself and equalizing the playing field by setting boundaries is healthy. Proudly disrupt the distortion that sensitivity is the problem.

Being shamed for being sensitive or empathic isn't and should never be "normal" or "okay". I also want to remind you to always use your best judgment in each situation. If someone is making you feel unsafe with their words or actions, or you're in danger, ensure your safety first.

There's also wisdom in choosing your battles. One strategy I have for choosing battles is that, after I ground and process on my own, I ask myself on a scale of 1-10 how much something is still bothering me. If it's 6 or higher, this is usually when asking for a conversation with a person feels appropriate.

I have found that most people appreciate opportunities to clear the air, especially when you start a conversation with a heartfelt intention. A talk isn't always the answer for me. Sometimes I feel it best to reduce contact with the person, write a cathartic journal entry or other solutions come to me.

That being said, this book is to help those who choose to speak up. Now, a quick look at the anatomy of an insult, so you feel further supported in setting boundaries around sensitivity shaming.

PART 3

ANATOMY OF AN INSULT

Statements often have explicit and implied messages. For example, we probably all know that pesky relative who's asked you (maybe 100 times): "When are you going to get married?". Part of the reason people dislike questions like this has to do with the implicit messages.

Explicitly, it's a presumptuous and nosy question. On an implicit level, it contains all kinds of messages. Such as the expectation that you should be married or something is wrong because you aren't (shaming). It also implies it's the person's business and they get input on how you live your life.

So what are the implied messages when someone calls you "overly sensitive"? They include: *You should be less sensitive. You're being difficult. The problem is you and your sensitivity.* Moreover, it implies that the person commenting thinks they get to decide who and how you are - Which they don't. In short, you're not imagining things if people make this comment, and it feels off-color.

Heaven forbid you stretch someone's consciousness with your inconvenient sensitivity. Consciousness is, by and large, a progressive quality. If there's ever been a war that was started because someone was too sensitive, I'd like to know.

All this is said to support your mindset and confidence around setting boundaries. This is important because the energy you bring to the interaction can make all the difference. You and sensitivity are worthy of respect.

10 RESPONSES TO BEING CALLED "OVERLY SENSITIVE"

Imagine someone just called you "overly sensitive"...again. Instead of stalling and ruminating about it for years, I invite you to visualize yourself calmly making a new choice, as your sensitive warrior self. See it going well. Remember your powerful, baby-making voice and your valuable gift of sensitivity. We're all equals, and it's important to set boundaries that let others know what is and isn't okay.

Warriors come in different frequencies. There are no nonsense ones, funny ones, unconditionally loving ones, fiery ones, and more. I suggest you experiment with which frequencies resonate with you, in different situations.

In addition to coming from as grounded a place as possible, I suggest you always add the energy of love or blessing to what you say, or at least intend to.

If "grounding" is new to you, it's like how it sounds. When you meet someone who seems "down to earth", you feel they are present and centered. These are qualities of being energetically grounded as well. In short, it means to be present in your body and anchored in the support of the earth, as the earth also anchors into you supporting her.

One easy way to do this is to feel your feet on the ground, or your clothes on your skin if your feet bring up discomfort. Then visualize roots going from the bottoms of your feet into the earth. I like to have them reach into earth's core and feel the earth's energy naturally arise up my body. It's a great daily practice.

Each of these 10 responses is followed by a brief note about it, so that if it doesn't resonate with you, you have a foundation to string your own words together. Some of the notes contain responses that might suit you better (you're getting more than 10!). Generally speaking, the list starts with more casual comments, and ends with ones that are more appropriate for closer relationships.

I wrote this with in-person interactions in mind (not text or social media, though they're adaptable). I also wrote them with personal rather than business situations in mind. The final decision is always yours. Please be a responsible voice parent and use your best discernment for your particular situation. Tone is an important part of the picture too.

Sensitives can have a lot of sass and joy. These are traits that go a long way. Don't be afraid to make light with your light, and let those qualities shine through in your boundary setting. In other situations, you may feel you need to be more firm.

Now for the 10 responses. Drum roll...

1) "Overly sensitive" compared to what?

Reminds the person that labels are relative, and no one gets to decide how sensitive anyone ought to be. It's like asking, "What amount of sensitive should I be?" They're funny because they capture the ridiculousness of the premise. When I've said this, the other party has never had a response (at least, not one that made sense) and the shaming stopped.

2) I like being sensitive.

Self-acceptance is a powerful thing. This gives the message that there's nothing wrong with you, and you're shame Teflon®. It's another one that has stopped the shame attempt dead in its tracks.

3) I'm not over sensitive. You're under sensitive.

A comically feisty way to subvert the paradigm. You are not required to buy into the view that sensitivity is an inferior trait. You're reflecting the person's behavior back to them, and claiming your right to be. It also says, given that we are equals, from my point of view, you're insensitive. In seems to throw a monkey wrench into the shame apparatus.

4) I can tell you're not as sensitive. Let me know if I can help you with that.

Another humorous way to flip the script, and let your boundary be known. It truly is senseless to tell another human much they should feel. What's next, saying a person's eyes are too eyebally? In other news, cats purr too much. If you can see the humor in the response, you can probably make light of the comment.

5) Thank you. If you have further instructions on how to stop feeling, please let me know. I want to be a good robot.

A pinch of witt, a dash of truth. If you're human and you don't have feelings, there might be something wrong. Maybe in a realm where some people seem allergic to emotions, you're like spiritual anti-histamine.

6) Don't shame me.

A deft callout can be the simplest fix. A simple alternative might be: "Not cool". It's been said that the most predictable response to confrontation is denial. Some may respond with "I'm not shaming you". If you choose to speak to the denial, one possibility might be saying something like "I disagree, so please stop." The point is to reclaim your right to be the wonderful sensitive you are, and stand by your boundary.

7) Stop flipping this around.

Similar rationale as above. This is based on an occasion long ago when someone said something appallingly out of line to me. When I mentioned as much is when his shame attempt started, so it wasn't solely shaming. It was trying to offload accountability by saying it was me, and it was also gaslighting (which I consider a form of emotional abuse). This response is not unlike saying: "You just don't want to be called out." I believe avoiding accountability is actually one of the main reasons people sensitivity shame to begin with. Sometimes you need to put your foot down.

8) Why does sensitivity bother you?

The funny paradox of people calling you "overly sensitive" is that they appear to the the ones bothered. Not you. This response challenges the other person's bias, and keeps you in a shame-free zone. It can also spark a dialogue, which may be productive and clarifying.

9) I hear you think the problem is sensitivity. I disagree.

You don't have to agree with sensitivity shaming and blaming. This response addresses the blaming dynamic, which may help it shift. You're also maintaining your own space. An alternative might be: "This has nothing to do with sensitivity."

10) I feel (uncomfortable, mad, etc.) when you say that. It doesn't meet my need for (respect, acceptance, etc.). I'd like you to (stop the shaming/blaming, etc.).

The idea is to identify your emotion, and the unmet need behind it. Then make a request that would fulfill your need. This response is based on Nonviolent Communication (NVC) principles by Marshall Rosenberg, PhD. He does great work. It's obviously for more personally intimate situations, but don't be afraid to rock that gas station attendant's world with it.

Ta daa! **Bonus #11)** There's nothing wrong with being sensitive.

There's nothing wrong with being aware. There's nothing wrong with feeling. There's nothing wrong with being deep and intense.

One definition of shame is that it is the feeling/belief that <u>you</u> are bad, whereas guilt is the feeling/belief that something you did was bad. This one nips all that in the bud. You can't argue with the truth of it.

You may have seen that social media meme that says something along the lines of: when people call you overly sensitive it means, you won't let me disrespect you. I think there's some truth to that.

Closing thought: If you can genuinely intend or beam unconditional love at the other person as you say these (or before or after), you win the teddy bear.

One of the greatest gifts and superpowers of sensitivity is that we're often willing to be real and deal with challenging things. When you can't help but notice things, being willing to deal with them often seems to come with the territory. There are exceptions, but it truly is a strength.

In a society that isn't so skilled at dealing with unresolved issues and processing emotions, which can lead to all kinds of predicaments, sensitivity is a needed and valuable asset. Stop apologizing for it.

Case in point? One fascinating, well-known study on the health impacts of childhood abuse is the "Adverse Childhood Experiences" study (a.k.a. ACEs), conducted in 1998. It found a direct correlation between negative childhood experiences and chronic health conditions, addictions, early death and more. When it comes to healing, sensitives can be highly attuned to when something needs attention, and you can't heal what you don't notice. This is a great gift, to identify and bring light to issues, so that positive healing can occur.

Congratulations on birthing new life with your voice. Not sure what you put on a cake for that, but be sure to make a wish.

BAD CHINCHILLA

If there's a keynote for the responses, it's to be centered in your confident sense of self, with love and strength, and not take the shame-bait. As you know by now, this is why I've been doing my best to amp up your self-esteem throughout the book.

I aspire for you to feel confident. As if someone shaming your sensitivity was like calling you a bad chinchilla. You'd be like "Huh? I'm not a chinchilla. Did you fall off your chair at breakfast?" As if the other person isn't even seeing you clearly, because they're probably not.

The predominant level of planetary consciousness got us to where we're at today. It hasn't been such a great place. That's why I'm glad the world seems to be rapidly shifting. The way sensitives experience things often brings different and heightened awareness. We need that. We need out-of-the-box perspectives and ways to problem solve. In a way, only those outside the box can actually see the whole box.

One last time: High sensitivity is a beautiful and valuable trait. It has enabled me to care deeply, and be observant (I mean, when I'm not busy burning food or looking for the sunglasses perched on top of my head). Sensitivity can lead to unique creativity and perspective. I can be immersed in beautiful music and nature in a way that is vibrantly enriching. And it often means heartfelt connections with those I hold dear, especially animals.

There are other gifts and challenges that come with it. I invite you to start naming them in your own life. It can take a lifetime to learn how to best manage awareness and self-care when you're a sensitive and/or an empath. Always be kind and gentle with yourself on your path.

If I could flip the switch that made people stop sensitivity shaming and bullying I would, but I can't. There may always be people who aren't appreciative of what you bring. Remember that you are not the sum of other peoples' thoughts about you.

You are starlight. No matter what anyone says about starlight, it's always starlight. You might even start to feel genuinely bad for some people - That they don't appreciate the dreamy, lavish, crystalline gift of sensitivity.

Hopefully now you have a mindset and words to assert healthy boundaries when you deem appropriate. You deserve to be taken a stand for. You deserve to be your wonderful self. You are amazing just as you are.

Your sensitivity is honorable. Honor your sensitivity.

Now go forth, frolic and stay feisty.

ABOUT THE AUTHOR

Julia R. Wild is a bestselling author, spiritual teacher, and TEDxMileHigh blogger. She is also a writing and creativity coach for HSP, empathic and Indigo children and women, and a sensitive child consultant. She received her B.A. from Vassar College, and her M.S. Psychology *summa cum laude* from California Southern University. She is a cross-genre wordsmith. Her work been published in "Pink Panther Magazine" and a few other publications. Julia enjoys helping sensitives find their powerful voice. Find out more about her "Writing for Healing" workshops and join her email "Museletter" at https://www.juliarosewild.com.

ENDNOTES

David R. Hawkins, M.D., PhD., "Power Versus Force: The Hidden Determinants of Human Behavior." (California, Hay House, Inc., 2002) Elaine Aron, PhD, "The Highly Sensitive Person: How To Thrive When The World Overwhelms You" (New York: Broadway Books, 1997).

Felitti, V. J., Anda, R. F., Nordenberg, D., Williamson, D. F., Spitz, A. M., Edwards, V., . . . Marks, J. S. (1998). Relationship of childhood abuse and household dysfunction to many of the leading causes of death in adults: The Adverse Childhood Experiences (ACE) Study. *American Journal of Preventive Medicine, 14*(4), 245-258.

Hello Kitty® is protected by copyright and trademark. Sanrio®, Hello Kitty® and other Sanrio characters are trademarks of Sanrio Company, Ltd.

Marshall Rosenberg, PhD., "Living Nonviolent Communication: Practical Tools to Connect and Communicate Skillfully in Every Situation " (Colorado: Sounds True, Inc., 2012). Digital Book.

This book is intended and infused with uplifting, healing energy (for your highest good, according to you). To receive it, your conscious consent is needed. You don't have to, but if you would like it, you can intend to receive, consent to yourself or out loud, etc. You may or may not feel it right away (don't be discouraged if you don't).

You are reading the materialization of a dream come true. If you are laying eyes on this or holding it in your hands, I can't thank you enough for dreaming it with me. Never ever give up on your dreams. Ever.

* 9 7 8 1 7 3 4 5 2 9 9 2 0 *